YOUR KNOWLEDGE HAS VALUE

Antje Holtmann

War on Terror - How Discourse changed after 9/11

GRIN Verlag

Bibliografische Information der Deutschen Nationalbibliothek:

Die Deutsche Bibliothek verzeichnet diese Publikation in der Deutschen National-
bibliografie; detaillierte bibliografische Daten sind im Internet über http://dnb.d-
nb.de/ abrufbar.

Dieses Werk sowie alle darin enthaltenen einzelnen Beiträge und Abbildungen
sind urheberrechtlich geschützt. Jede Verwertung, die nicht ausdrücklich vom
Urheberrechtsschutz zugelassen ist, bedarf der vorherigen Zustimmung des Verla-
ges. Das gilt insbesondere für Vervielfältigungen, Bearbeitungen, Übersetzungen,
Mikroverfilmungen, Auswertungen durch Datenbanken und für die Einspeicherung
und Verarbeitung in elektronische Systeme. Alle Rechte, auch die des auszugsweisen
Nachdrucks, der fotomechanischen Wiedergabe (einschließlich Mikrokopie) sowie
der Auswertung durch Datenbanken oder ähnliche Einrichtungen, vorbehalten.

Imprint:

Copyright © 2010 GRIN Verlag GmbH
Druck und Bindung: Books on Demand GmbH, Norderstedt Germany
ISBN: 978-3-656-40299-2

This book at GRIN:

http://www.grin.com/en/e-book/211626/war-on-terror-how-discourse-changed-
after-9-11

GRIN - Your knowledge has value

Der GRIN Verlag publiziert seit 1998 wissenschaftliche Arbeiten von Studenten, Hochschullehrern und anderen Akademikern als eBook und gedrucktes Buch. Die Verlagswebsite www.grin.com ist die ideale Plattform zur Veröffentlichung von Hausarbeiten, Abschlussarbeiten, wissenschaftlichen Aufsätzen, Dissertationen und Fachbüchern.

Visit us on the internet:

http://www.grin.com/

http://www.facebook.com/grincom

http://www.twitter.com/grin_com

E.-M.-Arndt-University of Greifswald

English Department

Discourse Analysis WS 2009/10

War on Terror -

How Discourse changed after 9/11

by Antje Hübner, 3rd Semester,

LA Gym Englisch, ev. Religion, DaF

Date: 26.4.2010

Introduction

When George W. Bush delivered his State of the Union Address on September 21, 2001, the media spoke of "the most important speech of his life and also one of the most important addresses of a president to a joint session of Congress for half a century"[1] as one can find in *BBC News*. *The Time* even describes his speech as "the finest, strongest, clearest, several-times-chill-giving speech of his life"[2]. Eighty-two million people watched Bush's speech, which is considered to be "the year's largest television audience save the Super Bowl"[3] Before his outstanding speech, Bush was "routinely mocked for his linguistic shortcomings"[4] as Kevin Coe (et al.) writes in *No Shades of Gray*. Coe et al. also mention that the media praised Bush's "steel and eloquence"[5] and his "clear rhetorical power"[6] afterwards.

The discourse he (re)started, continued or resumed on "shaped public discussion and debate surrounding terrorism worldwide"[7]. '9/11' has become a term everybody understands "in its conventional sense, as a realm of creative expression"[8] as Daniel J. Sherman and Terry Nardin point out in their book *Terror, Culture, Politics: Rethinking 9/11*. Also Shana Kushner and Amy Gershkoff say that '9/11' has become an "ideograph in the sense that the historical event represents an attack on the beliefs, values, attitudes and "way of life" within the United States"[9]. Not only in the English language '9/11' has become a "dictum"[10] but in many others, too.

In this term paper I want to take a closer look on the speech President Bush delivered on September 20, 2001 as State of the Union Address to a joint session of Congress. In my analysis I will go through the speech step by step in order to figure out the main points Bush is making. From there I want to continue with its effects and influence on the discourse about 'war on terror'. I am mainly referring to Norman Fairclough and his interpretations in *Language and Globalization* and also to Kevin Coe et al. and their study *No Shades of Gray*. With the help of these publications I

---

[1] http://news.bbc.co.uk/2/hi/americas/1555912.stm, checked March 23, 2010
[2] http://www.time.com/time/nation/article/0,8599,175757,00.html, checked March 24, 2010
[3] Coe. Kevin, et a.: No Shades of Gray, p. 240
[4] Coe. Kevin, et a.: No Shades of Gray, p. 234
[5] Coe. Kevin, et a.: No Shades of Gray, p. 234
[6] Coe. Kevin, et a.: No Shades of Gray, p. 234
[7] Hodges, A., Nilep, C.: Discourse, war and terrorism, p. 1
[8] Sherman, Daniel J., Nardin, Terry: Terror, Culture, Politics: Rethinking 9/11, p. 1
[9] Kushner, Shana. and Gershkoff, Amy. "The 9/11-Iraq Connection: How the Bush Administration's Rhetoric in the Iraq Conflict Shifted Public Opinion", http://www.allacademic.com/meta/p82590_index.html, checked March 23, 2010
[10] Source: http://www.spiegel.de/spiegel/print/d-48753340.html, checked March 23, 2010

want to emphasize the impact and the aftermath of Bush's discourse as well in media as in society.

Analysis of the speech

Bush's speech contains about 3000 words. It is striking that he uses the words 'terror'/'terrorists'/'terrorism' about twenty-four times. Other important keywords are 'freedom' and 'justice' and on the other side 'war', 'al Qaeda', 'Taliban' and also 'Afghanistan'. It is significant that Bush refers to 'America'/'US' c. thirty-eight times and addresses the people he with "my fellow Americans".

Every quote I am referring to is taken from the transcript of *President Bush's address to a joint session of Congress on Thursday night, September 20, 2001*[11] as published on CNN.com.

In his introduction Bush addresses the Speaker, the President Pro Tempore and the members of Congress first, which are considered to be the highest officials in the United States of America. He then addresses the American people by saying "fellow Americans". Bush points out that it is an abnormal occasion and that the State of the Union he is going to speak on "has already been delivered by the American people". He goes on and explains what happened on September 11 and already uses the word 'terrorists' in his first sentences.

To show inner connection and sympathy for the people, he names two citizens, Todd Beamer, a passenger and is wife Lisa Beamer. The audience reacts with an applause. He then describes the situation and what is happening in the USA and also around the world and uses anaphora constructions, e.g. "We have seen" and "We will not forget". The use of the plural takes everybody in and creates some kind of unity. Also when Bush addresses the American people again by saying "my fellow citizens" this unity is established. Clearly, Bush has the world perspective in mind when he makes mention of "the entire world" and underlines the widespread influence of the attacks. He is especially referring to Great Britain as true friend and welcomes the British prime minister, which is somewhat important for the politic relations.

Already in the introduction one can find the dichotomy, which Bush creates throughout his whole speech, as he contrasts "enemies" with "justice" and "freedom", which is one of the main values in the American society. Bush makes clear that although "Americans have known wars" and surprise attacks, which he points out

---

[11] Source: http://archives.cnn.com/2001/US/09/20/gen.bush.transcript/, checked on March 24, 2010

three times, but nothing like the attacks of September 11. With his statement that there is a "different world" now, the enormity of the attacks is exposed one more time. Besides the introduction, Bush's speech is built upon four leading questions. Though they are rhetorical questions, which Bush answers himself, they address the American people directly and take everybody in so that everybody feels addressed. His first question is "Who attacked our country?"and from there Bush goes into the subject concerning al Qaeda and the Taliban. He mentions Osama Bin Laden and gives the al Qaeda organization a face. He highlights al Qaeda as the terrorist group and compares it with the mafia. Bush also links terrorists to "Islamic extremism" and, moreover to "evil and destruction". As a prime example he mentions Afghanistan and explains the situation is this country. An important rhetorical step is that Bush distinguishes between the Taliban and the people of Afghanistan by saying "The United States respects the people of Afghanistan (…) but we condemn the Taliban regime". He then makes five absolute demands on the Taliban, which should show power, influence and independence of the USA. Again the audience responds with an applause.

At this point Bush sets an antipol by emphasizing that the Islamic faith is respected and he even concedes that "its teachings are good and peaceful" and mentions that it is practiced in many countries "America counts as friends". Having said that, Bush makes clear that "terrorists are traitors to their own faith" and defines the "enemy" as the "radical network of terrorists". Considerably, he says that the enemy is neither the "many Muslim friends" nor "the many Arab friends". Again one can find dichotomy here, where Bush contrasts "enemy" with "friend". After another applause at this point, Bush mentions the term "war on terror" for the first time.

The next question Bush is asking in representation of the American people is "Why do they hate us?". Bush gives the following reason: "They hate our freedoms.". And again he points to dichotomy by distinguishing between "them" and "us". By saying "We have seen their kind before" Bush realizes that this situation is not new to the USA and in a historical perspective he adds "terrorists to a grisly Murderer's Row of history"[12].

The third question "Americans are asking" is "How will we fight and win this war?". Bush points out that everything will be done to defeat terrorism. He refers to former military action, for example in Iraq and Kosovo and explains at the same time how this war will be different. While he prepares the American people for it, he also saves

---

[12]http://www.time.com/time/nation/article/0,8599,175757,00.html, checked on March 24, 2010

them from false expectations. What follows is the central declaration and the peak of Bush's speech: "Either you are with us or you are with the terrorists". Bush leaves no room for alternatives here and also reaches the peak of the his concept of dichotomy. Another important point he is making here is the self-awareness that America is "not immune from attack", from which Bush's decision results to build the Office of Homeland Security. In the following he presents its function and introduces Tom Ridge, who will lead it.

Bush refers again to the bigger picture, not only considering America, but the world by saying that "this is not, however, just America's fight. (…) This is the world's fight. This is the civilization's fight". He shows that everybody is involved in this fight, because it is a fight for common values, such as "pluralism, tolerance and freedom". Bush even seems to act on the assumption that, as he says, "the whole world is rallying to America's side".

The last question he asks is "What is expected of us?" and gives marching orders in the last paragraph of his speech. First he gives an answer, which is very pleasing and American people wanted to hear. He simply says "(...) live your lives and hug your children" and "uphold the values of America". He repeats that it is a "fight for principles". In the last paragraph Bush even mentions the comforting power of prayer. He goes on with thanksgiving to the American people and also to Congress. After expressing what he expects from the American people, Bush exposes what the Congress will do and uses the anaphora construction "we will come together" five times. To follow his concept of dichotomy, he contrasts the "age of terror" with the "age of liberty" in his view to the future. Bush then explains that "freedom and fear are at war" by using the terms as personification.

Towards the end of his speech Bush suggests to "go back to our lives and routines" and points out that it is good to do so. But what he also underlines is, that "each of us will remember" and again he names a particular person, here George Howards, who died at the World Trade center. One more time Bush creates a lot of empathy here, because he shows a picture of George Howard, which his mother gave to him.

After exposing what the American people should do and what the government will do, he closes by saying what he will do. He also repeats that "freedom and fear, justice and cruelty have always been at war" and refers to God, who "may (…) grant us wisdom" at the very end of his speech.

War on terror – a closer look

Speaking of discourse of 'war on terror', it is important to define the term 'terror' at first. In his book *Language and Globalization* Norman Fairclough gives the following definition for it: "the immediate human victims of violence are chosen randomly or selectively from a target population, and serve as message generators"[13]. He also says that "terrorism is only one part of long-term shift of violence and war"[14] and refers to it as "irregular warfare"[15] and even labels it as a "catch-all category"[16]. Besides this definition taken from Schmid's *Political Terrorism* Fairclough also makes mention of the definition the UK Terrorism Act of 2000 established. He says this definition "is quite close to everyday usage of the word 'terrorism'"[17]. It reads: "the use or threat of action (…) designed to influence the government or to intimidate the public for the purpose of advancing a political, religious or ideological cause"[18].

Fairclough mentions three constructive effects of the discourse of "war and terror", i.e. "it construes terrorism in a particular way (…), implementation of discourse includes military actions against 'terrorism' (...) and constructs it as real object" so "contemporary terrorism can be seen as produced and as effect of the war on terror"[19]. His view on the attacks from September 11 is plain. He says that the USA as imperialist power with increasing militarism has led to opposition, which only found its most dramatic expression in the attacks from September 11.

Fairclough exposes the main themes of the discourse of the 'war on terror' and I want to name two of them, which I consider most important for this paper. The first thing he mentions is the "new era"[20]. Although terrorist attacks were not new, it is said that "things will never be the same again"[21] after September 11. Bush points out "the symbolic significance of the attack being centred upon the World Trade Center"[22]. In contrast, Fairclough says that is not epoch-changing, but more an event in a process because "al-Qaida has been targeting America since 1991"[23]. What Fairclough exposes is that the event became epoch-changing "because it was (…) represented

---

[13]Fairclough, Norman: Language and Globalization, p. 142
[14]Fairclough, Norman: Language and Globalization, p. 142
[15]Fairclough, Norman: Language and Globalization, p. 143
[16]Fairclough, Norman: Language and Globalization, p. 152
[17]Fairclough, Norman: Language and Globalization, p. 152
[18] Fairclough, Norman: Language and Globalization, p. 152
[19]Fairclough, Norman: Language and Globalization, p. 143
[20]Fairclough, Norman: Language and Globalization, p. 144
[21]Fairclough, Norman: Language and Globalization, p. 144
[22]Fairclough, Norman: Language and Globalization, p. 144
[23]Fairclough, Norman: Language and Globalization, p. 145

in this way by politicians and officials"[24], which was "important legitimizing move" including that "old truths and assumptions may no longer apply, [and] we can expect things to be radically different"[25] in Fairclough's opinion.

The other main theme I want to show is what is called "forces of evil"[26]. While Bush speaks of 'evil acts' and in 2002 even of 'the axis of evil', Ronald Regan already formed this expression in the Cold War by calling the Soviet Union an 'evil empire'. This notice is also posited by Coe et al., who say Bush used "Cold War-tested binaries"[27], i.e. 'good' and 'evil'. Furthermore, Fairclough exposes that "representing the enemy has a history in the USA"[28] and it was not Bush's idea. But making use of it "can be an effective way of legitimizing extreme measures"[29] in the way that "violence can only be met by violence (...) [and] the only possible response to the evil of terrorism is war"[30] as Fairclough concludes.

The method of Binary Discourse

Fairclough says that "the world is implicitly divided into good and evil"[31] and speaks of binary division. Also Coe et al. broach the issue on binaries elaborately in their book *No Shades of Gray*. They say that "binary constructions are ideally suited for a U.S. Political culture dominated by mass media"[32]. The definition they give for binary is "the placement of one thought or thing in terms of its opposite"[33]. They also mention that "Western language and thought often represent the world as dichotomized, absolutes consisting of antithetical terms and ideas, with no alternative ground"[34] and that "such constructions gain great political importance when employed within a strategic discourse that contains three attributes seemingly present in the Bush administration's post-September 11 communications"[35].

Fairclough says "it is taken for granted that America is on the side of the good"[36] and that there is "no space for those who oppose US policies in political rather than

[24]Fairclough, Norman: Language and Globalization, p. 145
[25]Fairclough, Norman: Language and Globalization, p. 145
[26]Fairclough, Norman: Language and Globalization, p. 146
[27]Coe, Kevin et al.: No Shades of Gray, p. 236
[28]Fairclough, Norman: Language and Globalization, p. 146
[29]Fairclough, Norman: Language and Globalization, p. 147
[30]Fairclough, Norman: Language and Globalization, p. 147
[31]Fairclough, Norman: Language and Globalization, p. 151
[32]Coe, Kevin et al.: No Shades of Gray, p. 235
[33]Coe, Kevin et al.: No Shades of Gray, p. 235
[34]Coe, Kevin et al.: No Shades of Gray, p. 235
[35]Coe, Kevin et al.: No Shades of Gray, p. 235
[36]Fairclough, Norman: Language and Globalization, p. 151

violent ways"[37]. He alludes that the polarization between good and evil has a dangerous moment, because "there are no third (or fourth) categories"[38]. Fairclough concludes "that the recent wars have actually strengthened [terrorism]"[39].

As I have already mentioned, Bush contrasts 'good' to 'evil', which is called a binary construction. Such binary discourse has three attributes according to Coe et al. First they say binary discourse "requires a central organizing object that provides a foundational meaning to the surrounding language and emphases"[40] as Coe et al. expose in *No Shades of Gray*. Furthermore, they explain that this object "might be a behavior (e.g. abortion), an idea (e.g., communism), or an event (e.g., September 11)"[41]. It is important that "the audience [has] strong beliefs"[42] and that there is "an interpretation perceived as widely shared about the object"[43]. Coe et al. expose that the attacks from September 11 provided such an object, which "President Bush centrally employed in a strategic binary discourse"[44].

The second attribute is that binary discourse is liable to "a particular ordering of discourse"[45]. What is also indispensable to Coe et al. is that "binary discourse must have an establishment phase, during which a speaker does two things: (a) initiates or substantially increases the usage of binaries, and (b) employs the binaries in a rhetorically notable manner"[46].

During the continuous discourse "a speaker can periodically repeat (or nearly so) the binary"[47] or can "consistently highlight the concepts on either side of the binary"[48].

The final attribute that Coe et al. make mention of is that binary discourse utilizes multiple binary constructions"[49], which means they "allow a speaker to make strategic decisions and respond to multiple exigencies, such as emphasis upon a particular binary to fit a specific need"[50].

Coe et al. mention two benefits that Bush carries away. The first one is that "binaries can serve the function of "unification by a foe shared in common [and] utilization of

[37]Fairclough, Norman: Language and Globalization, p. 151
[38]Fairclough, Norman: Language and Globalization, p. 151
[39] Fairclough, Norman: Language and Globalization, p. 161
[40]Coe, Kevin et al.: No Shades of Gray, p. 235
[41] Coe, Kevin et al.: No Shades of Gray, p. 235
[42] Coe, Kevin et al.: No Shades of Gray, p. 235
[43]Coe, Kevin et al.: No Shades of Gray, p. 235
[44]Coe, Kevin et al.: No Shades of Gray, p. 236
[45]Coe, Kevin et al.: No Shades of Gray, p. 236
[46]Coe, Kevin et al.: No Shades of Gray, p. 236
[47]Coe, Kevin et al.: No Shades of Gray, p. 236
[48]Coe, Kevin et al.: No Shades of Gray, p. 236
[49]Coe, Kevin et al.: No Shades of Gray, p. 236
[50]Coe, Kevin et al.: No Shades of Gray, p. 236

these two likely helped to unify the U.S. Public - initially against terrorists"[51]. Secondly, the "use of these binaries helped to link the post-September 11 military campaigns to previous moments in U.S. history in which an enemy was more clearly defined (e.g. World War II)"[52].

Discourse and Media

Moreover, Coe et al. name to reasons why binaries fit into U.S. political culture. On one hand "binary oppositions inherently suggest competition between two forces"[53] and on the other hand they "are stylistically pleasing"[54]. They also have great moral power. It is striking that after September 11 media, especially newspaper editorials "aligned closely with President's Bush communications"[55]. This was increased through "patriotic sentiment and heightened security concerns that arose following the terrorist attacks"[56] as Coe et al. expose.

One of the most important binaries Bush uses throughout his entire speech is 'good' and 'evil'. Coe et al. did research in order to find out the increase of use of these words. Their results supported their expectations "that Bush initiated or increased his usage of the good/evil (...) in order to firmly establish these in U.S. political discourse"[57]. They found out that presidential paragraphs containing good/evil rose from 2.4% to 7.5%[58]. This, of course, influenced the media in such a way that the good/evil binary showed up in newspaper editorials with 26.8%, compared to 1.7%[59] prior. Coe et al. conclude that the results mark the "establishment phase of a strategic binary discourse by President Bush"[60].

In his State of the Union speech from September 21, 2001 Bush declares that "freedom and fear are at war" (Bush 2001b), which implies a battle between good and evil. It is appellative that the research by Coe et al. also shows how "editorials during this establishment period followed the president's use of these binaries"[61] by simply repeating Bush's words. I want o state two examples for this phenomenon.

---

[51]Coe, Kevin et al.: No Shades of Gray, p. 236
[52]Coe, Kevin et al.: No Shades of Gray, p. 237
[53]Coe, Kevin et al.: No Shades of Gray, p. 237
[54]Coe, Kevin et al.: No Shades of Gray, p. 237
[55]Coe, Kevin et al.: No Shades of Gray, p. 238
[56]Coe, Kevin et al.: No Shades of Gray, p. 238
[57]Coe, Kevin et al.: No Shades of Gray, p. 240
[58]Results taken from: Coe, Kevin et al.: No Shades of Gray, p. 241
[59]Results taken from: Coe, Kevin et al.: No Shades of Gray, p. 241
[60]Coe, Kevin et al.: No Shades of Gray, p. 241
[61]Coe, Kevin et al.: No Shades of Gray, p. 242

The first is taken from *Cleveland Plain Dealer,* which noted "George W. Bush has cast the war against international terrorism as a fight that pits 'good vs. evil'"[62] and another example is taken from *St. Louis Post-Dispatch,* which "echoed the president's dominant theme: "President George W. Bush gave the most powerful and important presidential speech in a generation Thursday night, summoning Americans and all the citizens of the civilized world to a war between 'freedom and fear'"[63]. Coe et al. discern from this that "when the language of the press so closely follows the discourse of the president, citizens and other political leaders"[64] automatically "interpret these editorials as a message of support for the president and his (...) agenda"[65].

To come back to the three categories and attitudes of discourse Coe et. al. summarize that on one hand "Bush's consistent references to the September 11 attacks indicate that he used these events as a central organizing object"[66] and on the other hand "the president ordered his binary communications in a strategic manner"[67] in means of increasing the usage of both binaries in a rhetorically strategic manner. Thirdly, one can find "presence of a particular ordering of discourse"[68], which make it memorable.

Conclusion

As discourse analysis "shifts the focus to the stories, the language, and the texts that create meaning"[69], it contains an "instability of meanings and the role of language"[70]. As one can see from the discussion, discourse changed significantly after September 11. The term '9/11' even became a dictum, which is known all over the world as synonym for the terror attacks and also as a hypernym for terrorism. The discourse since September 11 has "constructed reality, provided framework through which the world now views and discusses war and terrorism"[71]. The spread of the presidential discourse was mainly achieved and supported by media. Especially newspaper editorials, which gave exact citing of the president's utterances, played a huge role in

---

[62]Coe, Kevin et al.: No Shades of Gray, p. 242
[63]Coe, Kevin et al.: No Shades of Gray, p. 242
[64]Coe, Kevin et al.: No Shades of Gray, p. 246
[65]Coe, Kevin et al.: No Shades of Gray, p. 246
[66]Coe, Kevin et al.: No Shades of Gray, p. 246
[67]Coe, Kevin et al.: No Shades of Gray, p. 246
[68]Coe, Kevin et al.: No Shades of Gray, p. 248
[69]Discourse, war and terror, p. 11
[70]Discourse, war and terror, p. 11
[71]Discourse, war and terror, p. 13

this. While there was an increase of the use of 'good' and 'evil', the discourse was established in everyday life.

On the other hand discourse analysis can only give statistics. And although it "can analyze presidential speeches and examine language circulated among media", it is criticized that it cannot say what a "soccer mom shopping at Wal-Mart thinks about 9/11"[72].

Another important effect is that, eventually, the discourse "served as a discursive foundation upon which a number of policy goals were justified"[73], e.g. the Department of Homeland Security, as Coe et al. say. Lastly, Coe et al. underline that binary constructions have "ability to function as a powerful discursive strategy in U.S. Politics"[74], which George W. Bush made full use of and was no longer the incompetent but the brilliant speaker.

Bibliography

- Coe, Kevin; Domke, David; Graham, Erica S.; Lockett John, Sue; Pickard, Victor W.: *No Shades of Gray,*
on http://www.victorpickard.com/upload/NoshadesofGray..pdf
- Fairclough, Norman: *Language and Globalization.* London 2006
-Hodges, Adam; Nilep, Chad: *Discourse, war and terrorism.* Amsterdam/Philadelphia 2007
-*Kushner, Shana; Gershkoff, Amy: The 9/11-Iraq Connection: How the Bush Administration's Rhetoric in the Iraq Conflict Shifted Public Opinion,* on http://www.allacademic.com/meta/p82590_index.html
-Sherman, Daniel J.; Nardin, Terry: *Terror, Culture, Politics: Rethinking 9/11.* Indiana University Press, Bloomington 2006
-http://news.bbc.co.uk/2/hi/americas/1555912.stm
-http://www.time.com/time/nation/article/0,8599,175757,00.html
-http://www.spiegel.de/spiegel/print/d-48753340.html
-http://archives.cnn.com/2001/US/09/20/gen.bush.transcript/
-http://www.time.com/time/nation/article/0,8599,175757,00.html

---

[72]Discourse, war and terror, p. 11
[73]Coe, Kevin et al.: No Shades of Gray, p. 246
[74]Coe, Kevin et al.: No Shades of Gray, p. 249